Doyle Arts Inspirations

By Richard Doyle

Dedicated to
Matthew Doyle and Kathryn Doyle

Haiku

Time loans us seconds,
minutes, hours, days, a lifetime
tick, tock, tick, tock......tick

© Copyright 2017 by Richard Doyle of Doyle Arts. Richard Doyle retains the sole copyright to his contributions to the book.

All artistic renditions, revelations, and writings, including layout designs and graphic elements are copyrights of Doyle Arts 2017. DoyleArts.com

"Art is a legacy that all can leave."

That is a motto for which I've based my artistic career. I'm fortunate in that I have slowly uncovered some hidden artistic talents that I've tried to cultivate, and with a little hard work, a little luck, and a whole lot of help from people interested in my success, I've been able to live out my legacy.

I was not always an "artist", "poet", or "writer". In fact it's only been since 2010 that I actually felt comfortable with the personal label of "artist". It was at that time that I uncovered a niche in the artistic world through my watercolor collage paintings of historic towns, and universities. From there my art career took off as more and more people sought my collage art. As they learned more about me as an artist, they subsequently discovered my talents as a writer, and poet.

"You did that?" is a common response I hear from people who see my work, and who knew me in my younger years. That is normally followed by "I never knew you were an artist." Truth be told, neither did I. I was always an artistic kid, but never cultivated my talents. Frankly, I never had the time. My senior year in high school alone was packed full of playing three sports, and participating as a cast member in the fall play, and spring musical. Not quite the prototype of your typical aspiring artist. That's what makes my transition that much more fun as I tend to shock people with the divergence from the person they thought they knew.

I'm also a Financial Advisor as my "other" occupation. The whole "left brain versus right brain" topic seems to fascinate people as the analytical side battles the creative side. But it was actually through accomplishments in my financial career that led me to my start as an artist. It happened when I finally finished my thirteenth post-college exam for my financial planning advanced degree. On the way back from that last exam I decided to reward myself, so I stopped in a craft store and bought myself a set of paints. The rest, as they say, is history.

My art career took a giant leap forward when I was facing the most difficult challenges in my life. Some may even say that I was staring into the abyss. From that lowly place I painted my first collage. It was a painting of a small town called Sharon Center, Ohio for my mother-in-law as a Christmas gift. I had no money for gifts that year, and given that she had just lost her husband six months prior I was determined to do something special for her, so I made her a painting. The popularity of that collage led to other requests for neighboring towns, and special projects, and thus established me as a legitimate artist. The projects led to financial gains that I subsequently reinvested into my work, and thus slowly created what is now the growing legacy of Doyle Arts.

My art is now hanging in historic inns, universities, city halls, large corporations, civic entities, churches, and local museums. I've been featured in numerous newspaper articles, and have been on the covers of magazines, and books. It also landed me on a Public Broadcasting Services television special on the local art scene. It has also led to multiple speaking engagements, including a video of my work on the main stage of a national convention. All of these are things that I never could have imagined, but of which I am honored and grateful.

Along the way people emerged who helped me create my legacy. Looking back that legacy is a whole lot clearer now than it was when I was looking forward. But then again isn't that the beauty and mystery of life?

I owe a great deal of thanks and gratitude to artistic mentors, my family who rekindled my artistic career with some timely gifts, to the Medina County Art League who nurtured my talents and gave me opportunities to display my work, to the Medina Writer's Group who honed my writing skills, and to others who kept me pressing onward towards my goals. To all of these people I am truly grateful.

The beauty of my art and writings is that it has enabled me to offer so much "good" to so many people. My art has allowed me to raise tens of thousands of dollars for local charities, and to provide gifts which are truly one of a kind. At times I've had the privilege of providing a timely verse that may have comforted people in times of sorrow, or inspired them as they faced life's challenges. I've never looked at myself as an elite artist, rather just a person trying to leave a legacy of "good" in the world. My art and writings have allowed me the opportunity to do just that.

I hope you find inspiration in my art and writings. I hope it brings you as much pleasure as it has brought to me. I hope in the end it inspires you to also remember your own legacy, and perhaps inspire you to pursue your true calling. After all, "Art is a legacy that all can leave."

Warmest regards,

Richard Doyle
DoyleArts.com

The Answer

Shower your wisdom among paupers
It's not where I'm longing to be
As I aimlessly wander the meadows
In search of serenity

My silence is often questioned
As my intellect starts to wander
Through the valleys of life's riddles
Amid mountains of selfish squander

I long for something greater
The illusive cure for confused
As I joust with universal questions
Perhaps my illusionary muse

The answers flavor my lips
Like a rightly aged Chardonnay
More likely a fool's self-indulgence
God's humor for the day

For He is the only sentry
Holding keys to my inner doubts
And despite my selfish angst
Stays veiled in a perpetual shroud

So I'm called to trust His wisdom
And go peacefully dance in the fields
For once I stop seeking the answers
His answers may just be revealed

Haiku
  To form me like clay
would be useless; my hardened
soul requires chisels.

"Writer's Harvest"
  Thoughts are infertile seeds
until sown on parchment
and watered with ink,
bearing fruit for all.

Borrowed Blessings
(song)

The gift I got on my ninth birthday
Wore a ribbon on his head
Then he chewed up all my presents
That night he slept upon my bed
He was there for me
In the good and bad
Walked for years right by my side
I never knew how much I'd miss him
'Til the morning that he died

- chorus -
He was just a Borrowed Blessing
One of God's great gifts to me
Sometimes we think we own these moments
Only to find that we don't even hold the keys

She liked to wear pink ribbons in her hair
And he wore a crooked tie
It was picture time at school that day
And as the bus drove away I'd cry
And I was always there, made sure they combed their hair
But no matter how hard I tried
I couldn't keep them from growing older
And now they're taking my car to drive
(chorus) They were...

Now the trees seem so much taller now
The valleys a little deeper.
I'm moving much more slowly
And the stairs just a little steeper
Last year the girl I loved made her final climb
And as for me well, it's a matter of time
(continued)

Life is just a Borrowed Blessing
One of God's great gifts to me
Sometimes we think we own these moments
Only to find that He is holding all the keys

So treasure all the loves you find
For they might soon leave you behind
They're simply Borrowed Blessings
God's special gifts
His special gifts of time
They're simply Borrowed Blessings
God's special gifts
His greatest gift of time.

"Home"
  Wherever you roam, remember your home,
  For her memory will ensure you're never alone.

Dear Lord

Dear Lord:

It's me. I'm down here again struggling to believe. Just when I'm ready to call you a friend, it seems I'm abandoned, and back stabbed again.

I've given you chances. You've thrown them away. I invited you over, but you said "not today"! I'm tired of trying to bridge this gap, when all I get is shunned or slapped. I think it's time for my life to be autonomous.

Respectfully yours,
Anonymous

Dear Anonymous:

Oh, it's you again. And I'm the one who's called the false friend? How dare you question how I feel, the things I do, or the cards I deal.

You know the alternative, so go on your own, but rest assured you're never alone. For if you believe it's the end of the line, then all of my miracles were a waste of time.

I won't abandon you as you do me. Know that I'll be there in your hour of need. But deny me then, and then you'll see, your eternal partner won't be Me! You can't even imagine the horrors ahead. If you give up on Me you're already dead.

I feel so much pain that I'll continue to sob. Wishing you were here!

Love,
God

Haiku
  Believing in God
seemed so much easier when
He believed in me.

"Serving God"
  Serve God with the unique gifts with which He has served you.

"Jesus Wept" - 11 x 14 watercolor painting. Following some difficult events in my life there was a time when my faith drifted away. When it finally returned, I reflected upon how sad it must have been for Jesus to see that happen. I wanted to do something special, so I tried a finger painting, and "Jesus Wept" was the result. (2010)

Church on the Green

Tranquil and majestic
Her shadow is seen
Silently cast
Across the village green

For years she has witnessed
Families at play
Picnics and gatherings
On hot summer days

Generations of members
Supported her walls
As loyal church patrons
Answering His calls

A thriving community
She's guided through years
Of wars and depressions
She's comforted fears

Her doors were opened
As the hungry were fed
She quietly consoled
As tears have been shed

She has bid farewell
From God's green earth
And welcomed new life
Upon each child's birth

She'll continue to thrive
And her legacy will live
As long as there are those
Willing to give

Tranquil and majestic
Her shadow is seen
God bless the church
On the village green

Haiku
I can't change the world,
but I can change me, and that
just might change the world.

"Distant Goals"
Distant goals can sometimes be an optical illusion as they are often closer than you think.

"Church on the Village Green" - 22 x 30 watercolor painting. This century old church sits on the village green of Westfield Center, Ohio. One day while resting on the green I reflected on how many amazing life events were witnessed by the church, which became the inspiration of the poem "Church on the Green". (1999)

Peace

I release myself. I want no more
Turbulent waters eroding my shore.

I'll drift from bad, and focus on good.
Forgive all others, and do as I should.
I'll give for giving, anonymous is best.
Count my blessings, and long for less.

I'll pause for nature, and free my mind,
And never forget the gift of time.
I'll share my talents answering Your call.
Give unto others if ever they fall.

Carry a torch to illuminate Your light,
And never surrender the fight of good fights.
Though not deserving I beg for Your grace
In helping my soul to finish this race.

Like the hand You laid upon the restless seas
Calm these waters and grant me Thy…
Peace.

Haiku
   I have lost treasures
and wealth, but I lost the most
when I lost myself.

"Waves"
   Even the hardest rock
is softened by the most
persistent waves.

"Peace Lily" - 8 x 10 watercolor painting. One year I was asked what I wanted for Christmas. I simply replied "Peace". The Peace Lily's symbolism and beauty inspired this painting. (2010)

Circus Life

Life is a circus
A three-ring show
And you're the ringmaster
In the spotlight aglow
No matter the time
No matter your age
In the big top of life
You're always on stage

In time you'll tame a lion
A tiger, or a bear
In time you'll walk a tightrope
Disguising any fear
In time you'll be a juggler
Balancing your tasks
In time you'll seek the help
Of a strong supporting cast

At times you'll play the part
Of a sad circus clown
Wearing a painted smile
To cover a hidden frown
But in time you'll discover
A smile and a laugh
Will positively transform
Your spiritual path

As a performer in life
If ever you're down
Have the faith and a smile
Of a jovial clown
And push aside elephants
That stand in your way
Be like a traveling circus
And live for today

Haiku
*   Happiness is lost*
to those who persistently
shield themselves from it.

"Intoxicate"
*   Intoxicate on the spirits*
of laughter.

"Circus Life" - 11 x 14 watercolor painting. I was actually chosen from the audience to be a clown in a circus when I was a kid, and have always enjoyed clowns ever since. This painting was inspired by the poem "Circus Life" in which I reflect on how we all wear painted faces at times to hide our true emotions. (1999)

Perfect Line

The tides and seas will greet you
At the dawn of early life.
From a sheltered cove you'll venture
Along paths of ease and strife.

The sails upon your masts
Capture every wind benign.
So chart your course for greatness.
You'll sail the perfect line.

As you depart for open waters
Jagged shores will test your skill.
You'll battle villainous pirates.
Violent storms will test your will.

You'll venture beyond horizons
And push the tests of time.
So chart your course for greatness.
You'll sail the perfect line.

Before the sun's departure
As it sinks into the sea,
You'll encounter great adventures,
And discover your unique 'Me'.

Through trials and tribulations
In time you'll be just fine.
So chart your course for greatness.

You'll sail the Perfect Line.

Haiku
*When mud starts slinging
pigs will wallow, but only
fools choose to follow.*

*"Art"
One need not have
an eye for art,
To transform the soul,
or touch the heart.*

"Sail the Perfect Line" - 11 x 14 watercolor painting. Inspired from a song from a father to his son, in essence stating that regardless of what happens in life, if you stay true to yourself you will "sail the perfect line." It inspired my poem "Perfect Line". (1998)

First Summer Love

The senses of summer immediately came back
When I uncovered my mitt on an old garage rack.
The sights, the sounds, the feel of the leather.
The taste, the smell, the warmth of the weather.

I could smell the humidity, and oh how I'd lust
For the aroma of leather, popcorn and dust.
I could taste the dirt, and a big wad of gum,
Or the post game treats, we always had some.

The crack of the bat, coach yelling from third,
Mom and dad cheering, once again they were heard.
A weathered old bench, the feel of the grass,
The sting of the bat relived from my past.

I could see my old number and name on my shirt,
An umpire at home plate sweeping the dirt.
The senses came back with one "pop" of the glove.
Oh how I remember my first summer love.

Haiku
   A leopard in a
zebra-skin coat only hides
its spots for so long.

"Proud"
Whether a grin when you win,
Or a frown when you're down,
Nothing can replace
how loud I am proud!

<u>"Baseball Gear"</u> - 14 x 22 watercolor painting. I have had the privilege of coaching my son in baseball over many seasons. He learned many lessons along the way. Baseball is such a nostalgic sport that when I saw his gear leaning against the wall I had to capture it. The poem "First Summer Love" came from this painting and speaks to the five senses of baseball: sight, sounds, feel, taste, and smell. (2000)

Blanket of Gold

A Dandelion seed
makes its home

Wherever the wind
deems it to roam

For where it lands
and as it grows old

It's legacy will be
a blanket of gold

Haiku
*   Before the grapes dry*
on the vine, please take the time
to sample the wine.

"Forest"
*   From seeds to saplings,*
soon there's a forest.

Defeated

Defeated
Is not some arbitrary score.

Did I give it my all
Or could I've done more?

For the greatest of victories
Is not measured in feet,

But in facing the battles,
Not cowering in retreat.

When the game's end tolls
the scoreboard will say,

If I gave it my best,
It's a victorious day.

Haiku
    God paints us a bridge
to cross from dark times to light;
its called a rainbow.

"Boomerang"
    Throw out a
boomerang of kindness,
and then watch it
come back to you.

"Umbrella Abstract" - 14 x 22 watercolor painting. I was at a professional golf tournament when it started to rain just light enough for the players to continue to play, but it also brought out all of the spectators' umbrellas. I was amazed at the sea of blended colors in the gallery which inspired the painting. (2000)

Leaves of Life

Spring
A time when barren trees detonate into canopies of green.
With leaves individually exposed, yet strong in numbers.

Dutifully shadowing the sun, sheltering the rains, protecting the fowl.
Thriving in summer's serenity.

As autumn nears their inner beauty is exposed;
Striking in their color, uniquely their own, but oh for just a moment.

In time their vibrant hues can no longer shroud their brittle remains.
The strong grow weak, and the weak wisp away.

To those that remain the storms will assail.
The tightest of grips loosen each day.
The canopy of green is now a blanket of umber.

A few remain, deliberating their good fortune.
Among the remnants they feel alone.

Winter ascends, and surrender is near.
The last leaf falls, and signals the end.

Alas we are all but leaves in life.

Haiku
This is a haiku,
five - seven - five syllables,
but I ran out of.....

"Deep Roots"
The trees that weather
the fiercest storms,
Have the deepest roots
and strongest cores.

"Autumn Fishing" - 11 x 14 watercolor painting. While fishing in mid-autumn I captured this scene, along with a quote that I'll never forget from a friend, "Well I ain't catching no fish, but I sho' am catching a buzz." (2000)

One More Day

As the sun was setting
what would you say
if the rest of your life
was just one day?
Would you wish for things
in a material way,
reach out to friends,
or quietly pray?

Having it all
seemed the only way,
but I'd give it all up
for just one day.
That one last chance
so I might see
the special gifts
that made me "Me".

Like a toddler's hug,
or my lover's hands.
The unmistakable sound
of grade school bands.
My mother's perfume,
my father's style,
grandma's kitchen and
grandpa's smile.

The gift of charity,
the feel of pain,
the silence of dawn,
the summer rain.
Family gatherings,
or private tears.
A son's good humor,
a daughter's soft hair.

A dog's wet nose,
the miracle of a seed.
The compassion of others
in moments of need.
The roar of laughter,
the hush of a crowd.
An honest day's work,
and feeling so proud.

Toasting fond memories,
and learning to forget
the heartaches endured,
and all the regrets.
Finding my passion,
and one true love.
Finding forgiveness,
and the Lord above.

So much I discovered
as I traveled life's way.
What I wouldn't give for
just one day.

Haiku
   Facing fear reveals
that fear itself is faceless.
Bravery's conquered.

"Now and Then"
   If you feel now
that you missed too many "thens",
then refuse to miss any "nows".

One Good Eye

I was sitting on a bar stool
Drowning in my beer,
When I noticed from across the bar
An ol' timer's distant stare.
He had one eye on a photo,
and a bad eye behind a patch.
He looked as if he was longing.
From the world he seemed detached.

So I whispered to the barmaid,
"This next round, it's on me."
He toasted me from across the bar,
And said "Come sit by me."
So I made my way across the bar
and settled by his chair.
He said "My name is Thomas,
and this, my friend, is Claire."

A black and white old photo,
frayed along the sides,
Of a beautiful young lady,
flowing hair and pretty eyes.
"Forty years together,
My one and only love.
I prayed one day I'd find her.
She's my answer from above."

"Each night we spend together,
and dance the whole night through.
We talk until the sun comes up,
Nothing else we'd rather do."
And with that I saw a glistening
A tear in his one good eye.
He quietly got off his chair,
And tipped his cap goodbye.

A cane that had been hanging
On the coat rack across the floor,
Helped to steady his foot steps
As he shuffled out the door.
I yelled "Will I see you tomorrow?"
He grinned and gave a wink.
"Perhaps the good Lord willing,
and then I'll buy the drinks."
(continued)

"Can I ask just one more question,
before you leave tonight?
You seem to struggle walking,
So how do you dance all night?"

The old man paused a moment,
His head then bowed to the floor.
"Ahh a question worth repeating,
I've heard a thousand times before."

"You see my Claire, she died,
a few years back."
He said with a tearful sigh.
"So now when I want
to dance all night,
I just close my
one good eye."

"Storied Wines"
    Stories are like good wines: when you consume one from a great year, the bouquet is exquisite and the contents intoxicating.

Lost Friend

*Shattered remains
are concealed within
A fragile existence
behind camouflaged grins*

*Distant stares
from deadening eyes
Fails in vain
to conceal the lies*

*To me a disguise,
yet others can see
That I lost a friend,
and that friend is me*

Wishes

*I made a wish.
It didn't come true*

*So in regards to wishes
I think I am through*

*But then alas
it occurred to me*

*that perhaps a 'prayer'
is the wish I need*

Haiku
  The altruists of criticism are rarely willing receivers.

"Candor"
  The difference between candor and meddling is the person offering the opinion.

"Savannah" - 18 x 22 watercolor painting. Inspired from a scene of one of the historic town squares surrounding Savannah, Georgia. (1999)

The Look in Our Eye

They claimed their victory with an ominous lead.
The looks on their faces were of arrogance and glee.
Hoisting a trophy, or so they assumed.
Interviews in the awning, but in the background we loomed.
"Bring on the next", before game's end they'd cry.
But they forgot one thing,
the look in our eye.

We fell behind quickly, exhausted and gassed.
Our hopes for a victory, for others soon passed.
But something was brewing deep down inside
A brotherly spirit, a fiery pride.
They all had assumed we'd lay down and die.
But they forgot one thing,
the look in our eye.

We battled with grit, left our hearts on the floor.
With nothing remaining, but the game's final score.
Counting us out, was their biggest mistake.
For the victor's trophy was not theirs to take.
A championship banner they thought they would fly.
But they forgot one thing,
the look in our eye.

(Continued)

A lesson in life they'd not soon forget:
While the weak may cower, the strong never quit.
Premature donning of their "Champions" smock,
Was not theirs to wear with time on the clock.
From the depths of defeat to victory's high.
They'll always remember,
the look in our eye.

Dedicated to "The Miracle of Medina"
1983 Medina High School Basketball Team

"Medina Justice" - 17 x 21 watercolor painting. A view of the old courthouse (1841) and the new courthouse on the square of Medina, Ohio. Originally painted back in 1998, and then "refurbished", it now hangs in Judge Dunn's chambers, who also grew up playing basketball with our team. (2010)

Biking in the Boondocks

Dodging crickets, dodging frogs,
Protect your legs from nipping dogs.
Startled horses, flattened snakes
Fresh black tar, and body aches.

Dodging puddles, dodging worms.
Dangerous gravel on corner turns.
Bugs in eyes, bugs in teeth,
Uphill climbs, potholes beneath.

Dodging joggers, dodging storms,
Roadside litter, buzzing swarms.
Red Winged Blackbirds, baby hares,
Rusty nails, and Wooly Bears.

Chains fall off, sweat in eyes,
Fatigue sets in, burning thighs.
Country bike rides I must say,
"Whose idea was this anyway?"

Haiku
My mirror shouts "Fraud",
and when confessed to the world
she shouts back "Us too."

"Ripples"
The clearest reflection
in the calmest waters,
can be blurred from the ripple
of the slightest alter.

"Root Road Bridge Ashtabula County" - 11 x 14 watercolor painting. Painted as a charitable donation to help restore the 18 covered bridges of Ashtabula County, Ohio. (2010)

Wink Moments

Life is full
of those unique times
When alas you cross that proverbial line.

A prank, a kiss,
or a venial sin,
When wrong was wrong, yet still you grin.

When bad felt good
and the devil got the tilt.
And you felt bad for not feeling the guilt.

Where only a few
know what your mind's eye thinks,
When the moment's relived with a smile and a wink.

As the years go pass
and the memories gray,
Those special "wink moments" will never fade.

So live out those days
each chance you get.
And make life an adventure you won't soon forget.

Haiku
   When you lose something,
on occasion it returns.
Trust is rarely one

"Dream Garden"
   Plant a seed of vision,
   throw a little failure on it,
   water it with hard work,
   add some positive sunshine,
   and watch your dream grow.

"Wheelbarrow" - 14 x 19 watercolor painting. The painting was inspired by an old roadside wheelbarrow outside of an Amish farm in Holmes County, Ohio in the heart of Amish-Country. (1998)

Blink of an Eye

In a blink of an eye
A baby's cry
Toddler's drool
Off to school
Tying laces
Expensive braces
First car date
Graduate
Start a career
Marry your dear
One on the way
Hair turns gray
Kids move on
Retirement dawns
Grandkids play
Health soon fades
Fragile falls
Good Lord calls
Loved ones cry
In a blink of an eye.

Haiku
    Lack of tolerance
for intolerance is in
fact intolerance.

"Risk"
    Risking nothing is often
risking it all.

"Gazebo Flowers" - 13 x 21 watercolor painting. Captures a floral interpretation of the Medina, Ohio gazebo located on the Uptown Square. Painted as a charitable donation to the CFC Foundation (Cardio-Facio-Cutaneous) to help raise money for my nephew with special needs. (2004)

Artist Eyes

His eyes they'd see a mountain
That wasn't really there
Or a strand of auburn color
on a lock of golden hair
And reflections that blinded others
To him were diamonds bright
And when others stared at darkness
His eyes could see the light
Through artist eyes
Through artist eyes

Time can heal the heartaches
But sometimes not the pain
When the world longs for sunshine
It often gets the rain
Yet dark clouds on the horizon
Are always followed by sun
When brush strokes work their magic
And the colors start to run
Through artist eyes
Through artist eyes

His canvas was a mirror
Of a world his eyes could see
And God made him a vessel
That could put it down for me
But now sits in the corner
A canvas of empty white
For now my eyes see darkness
Because his now see the light
Through artist eyes
Through artist eyes

Haiku
To exacerbate
inequality just scream
"Inequality!"

"The Path"
If God made me a vessel
With talents for all to see
Then who am I to question
The path He's set for me?

"Marilyn Monroe Scribble Art" - 22 x 18 Magic Marker scribbled on watercolor paper. The artist starts with an underlying gray marker, followed by black marker, and just a touch of color. The poem "Artist Eyes" was written for a funeral of a local artist who donated his eyes to a lucky recipient. What a blessing for some stranger to receive the eyes from an artist. (2012)

True Friend

I gave of me
yet it wasn't returned
I offered my hand
to which it got burned

I sacrificed myself
but soon shunned aside
I offered my truths
to my face they all lied

I gifted my secrets
to others they'd tell
My heart now a fortress
my surface a shell

Yet despite all the others
I'm blessed in the end
For God took my hand
when He made you my friend

Haiku
   Friendship's not hidden agendas or goals, rather serendipity

"Dragonfly"
   When spying a dragonfly dancing on air,
   Your Guardian Angel is hovering near.

"Dragonfly" - 7.5 x 10 watercolor painting. A painting inspired by a story of how guardian angels appear to us as dragonflies. It was painted for a friend. (2009)

Dear Mother

Dear Mother,
How can I tell you
How much you mean to me,
When all these years I've hidden
The words so selfishly?

So as I sit and ponder
The words to honor you,
I find them not in verse,
But in following in your shoes.

For your time is not your own,
Yet never a word, or complaint.
You share in all my joys.
Comfort in times of rain.

Your joy is not a destiny
In some far distant place,
But rather a life-long journey.
Each day a smiling face.

Your commitment never waivers.
Your loyalty never contrived
Yet selfishly I hide away
My admiration deep inside.

But when I think of who I am
And the gifts that I've been given,
I see a mirrored image of
The life that you've been living.

For when God sent down His only Son
To walk upon the Earth,
He did so through the gift of life,
And a loving Mother's birth.

He could have sent an army,
But an army often yields.
He wisely chose a Mother,
His greatest protective shield.

So for all the time I've wasted
In never expressing my love,
You're everything I long to be,
God's Angel from above.

Haiku
   Maddening artists
are not haunted by life, but
by missing brush strokes.

"Rich Kids"
   From the lap of luxury
rich kids aren't born,
For a lap of a mother
is where riches are formed.

"Bailey Girl Giraffe" - 11 x 14 watercolor painting. Painted for a young lady named Bailey, who managed to work her way through some very difficult times through the help of her loving mother. This painting represents the bond between a mother and a daughter, and is one of my most popular paintings. (2007)

Coach

They came with eager hearts
To play a game they love,
Brandishing their uniforms,
Baseball bats, and gloves.
Eager to learn, they had no skills,
They could not hit or run.
Until with patience and some care,
You taught them to have fun.

At times they lacked attention,
They giggled, or they cried.
At times you watched in marvel,
As they hit, or caught pop flies.
At times you had to holler,
Drop the flowers or the dirt
At times you lent a hand,
To wipe a tear if they got hurt.

The score it never mattered,
As long as they played their best.
Giving their all and having fun,
Would pass the "winners" test.
Through faded years and grayer hair,
A champion you may not boast.
More important in the hearts of all the kids,
You'll forever be their
"Coach"!

Haiku
  *Defeat is erased
when external efforts meet
internal desire.*

"Art of Life"
  *Your heart is a pallet,
your deeds its canvas.*

"Little Fella" - 14 x 22 watercolor painting. Portrait of my two-year old son wearing my Cleveland Indians ball cap as we were preparing to watch the Indians in their first World Series game, the first to take place in over 50 years back in 1995. (1998)

I've Had My Day

It's come to pass
I've had my day
I've touched some hearts
along the way
I've lifted spirits
and succumbed to fears
Shared some laughter
and shed some tears

I've battled the wicked
and defended the good
Cowered at times
 and at times I stood
I've taken some hits
and dished some out
Maintained my faith
through times of doubt

Held winner's banners
and loser's shame
Honored my family
and disgraced my name
Commanded attention
and challenged my mind
Tested some boundaries
and crossed some lines

I had true wealth
yet thought I was poor
Gave as if Jesus
 was there at my door
Taken the blame
 for what others deserved
So maybe I'm not
 who you thought you observed

While not always perfect
 I still tried to be
My life is a legacy
 and my legacy is "Me"
As I reflect back fondly
 I'd have to say,
I'm the exception
 I've had my day

Haiku
   *Of the many wounds
suffered, none cuts deeper than
that of betrayal.*

*"Words to Live By"
   Trust, Honesty,
Loyalty, Respect:
All these things
your life should reflect.*

<u>"Garden Gate"</u> - 11 x 14 watercolor painting. Inspired by the Victorian gardens of yesteryears, painted in a way to draw the viewer into a peaceful scene and wonder what beauty awaits beyond the picket fence. (1998)

Badges

A secret world
is fully exposed
When badges appear
of purple and gold

Foolishly convinced
they're something deserved
With each broken dream
And each shattered nerve

Stoically you stood
as he handed them out
With each heavy blow
and each angry shout

You've taken his hits
and he's left his signs
Now leave while you can
you've done your time

Haiku
When religion is
worn upon a stranger's sleeve,
watch their other sleeve.

"Career"
To choose a career that's right for thee,
Start with the things you'd do for free,
And a life's ambition you just might see.

"American Waters" - 21 x 28 watercolor painting. Inspired by the historic victory of "Stars and Stripes" in the America's Cup yacht race against Australia. The blue of the United States flag acts as the blue of the ocean. (1999)

Be Yourself

Place your mask
up high on a shelf

And discover the joy
of being yourself

Stop trying to change
what others might see

For if you're not you
then who will be?

Haiku
*   Baby steps lead to*
minor tumbles and bruises.
Leaps lead to hard falls.

"Sharp Lessons"
*   The sharpest lessons in life are*
usually formed from the sharpest pains.

<u>"Daisies"</u> - 11 x 14 watercolor painting. While a complicated painting to pull off, it represents one of the simplest and most beautiful of flowers: the Daisy. There is always something "happy" about a daisy, which I tried to capture with the colors of the painting. (2001)

Opening Eyes

Are you walking down a path
that clearly you know,
is not the direction
or path you should go?

Praying to God
to finally reveal,
your purpose in life,
and not the surreal.

At times He whispers
and we may not hear,
but answers we seek
are probably near.

So before blaming Him
for ignoring your cries,
perhaps it is you
who should open your eyes.

Haiku
   People sometimes change,
not from their alterations,
but my acceptance.

"Ethics"
   Knowing" the right answer
isn't as difficult as "choosing" it.

"Hummingbird" - 11 x 14 watercolor painting. Very little in life can mimic the awe of spotting an illusive hummingbird as it feeds on the nectar of flowers. Inspired from a story of God's innocent messenger, I tried to capture the peace of this hidden imagery. (2009)

Volunteers

Smoke on the horizon.
The call comes down
A neighbor's in trouble in our quiet little town
From miles around the sirens they hear
On galloping horses come the Volunteers

They hitch up the pumper to the strongest of teams
With a crack of the reins it's off to the scene
With others on horseback, and gear in tow
Suspenders and helmets away they go.

They get there in time to dowse all the flames.
Our unsung heroes sheltered from fame
They work as a team for the good of us all,
While all risk some, and some risk all.

For those who have paid the ultimate cost
Of dying as heroes, and families who've lost,
And all those remaining, our heartfelt plea
"May the Lord watch over you
And grant you
Godspeed."

Haiku
    When extending hands to lift up a stranger, you also lift yourself.

"Failure"
Failure is knowing your true calling, and knowingly not following it.

<u>"Little Wiz"</u> - 15 x 22 watercolor painting. A collage of a local self-funded fire museum located in Medina, Ohio. Commissioned for the owner for his birthday, the museum is an example of how one man's passion can be a gift to others. (2010)

The Vault

Locked behind steel
are the pains of my past
Until the memories return
and steel turns to glass

Exposing the heartaches
of an imperfect world
And the myriad of nightmares
my mind has unfurled

There's so much to blame
and many at fault
I pray that the memories
go back in the vault

Permanently sealing
the bad ones away
And losing the key
so I can live for today

Haiku
Sometimes a closed gate may keep misfortune out, but locks good fortune in.

"Can"
To move into the world of "haves" from "have nots", You need to change your attitude to "can" from "cannot".

"Morning Delivery" - 22 x 30 watercolor painting. An abstract view of an early morning delivery to a local merchant on the historic Uptown Square of Medina, Ohio. The artist's kids initials are on the license plate. (1998)

Haiku
*   Until a heart's wound*
becomes a portal for grace,
love finds no refuge.

"Heron Poem" - 7.5 x 10 watercolor painting and poem. Original painting and poem combined together. The artist tried to capture a serene moment in the painting combined with his inspirational poem "You're Not Alone". (2010)

"Hummingbird Poem" - 7.5 x 10 watercolor painting and poem. The combination of the hummingbird and poem was discovered by a lady in California, who then purchased it for her mother who only had a few weeks to live. She said that her mother's final joys were to sit on the front porch watching the hummingbirds, and talking with God, and this was her daughter's final gift to her. (2010)

Bathtub Piranha

Stealth amid the calm reflected pool he anxiously awaits.
His prey approaches sheathed in satin and musk.

Gingerly she tests the water with polished toes,
As circular ripples announce her arrival.
Seemingly indifferent to the seething appetite that awaits her,
Her mischievous laughter accompanies her tottering submersion.

Pillowed amongst the clouds of suds she grins,
Neck feathered by auburn strands from a loosely braided bun.
Beads of condensation contour her face, as she
Wisps cumulous bubbles playfully from her hand.

Toying with her predator through the sultry steam,
Her eyes and smile transform into a ravenous hunger.
Roles are reversed; painted toes become her lance,
Not to defend, but to lure as if calling him into her snare.

His hunger turns to frolic, unabated bliss.
Water is displaced, as gentle waves transform into turbulent tides.

The Freshwater Piranha begins devouring his prey,

One succulent toe at a time.

Haiku
  Gossipers see all,
hear all, but rarely know all:
Truth reigns defeated.

"Seed's Belief"
When the weight of the earth
is thrust upon a seed,
she doesn't feel abandoned,
she grows and blossoms.

True Calling

I awoke this morning
and nothing had changed.
My life goals and realities
were clearly estranged.
The burdens I carry
seem a Pachyderm's load.
And the cards I've been dealt
make weaker foes fold.
But my destiny in life
is not fortune or fame.
Nor the world to know me;
on marquees my name.
Bequeath those to others
of selfish descent,
For a life of giving
is the life I was meant.
To lend a hand
to those who have fallen,
Is my badge of honor,
and my true calling.
So judge me not
by the wealth at life's end.
Judge me best
by the label "True Friend".

Haiku
   One need not seek out
true friendships, for in the end
true friendships seek us.

"Scandal of Grace"
To forgive and forget is the ideal place.
To forgive and recall is the scandal of grace.

One Inside

How do you tell a heart to turn and walk away,
From something truly special it's begging you to stay?

I think of all the people I've met along the way,
But few have ever captured me the way she does today.

With laughter deep and real, and a smile ne'er contrived,
Our conversations are fluid as the hours simply fly.

She'll never see her beauty through her humble eyes.
Yet every time I see her, my heart let's out a sigh.

A beacon from across the room her radiant smile and hair,
From others gets a passing glance; from me a lengthy stare.

And when she faces trials, I also feel her pain.
When the tears are flowing I'm standing in her rain.

The weight I see her carry down a rough and tumble road,
I long to lend a helping hand to help her ease her load.

At times I often wonder what her mind's eye thinks,
When tossing me a smile and getting back a wink.

She'll never see, or ever know the feelings that I hide.
I'll always see perfection for the one I keep inside.

Haiku
    Derivatives of
beauty are not external,
rather internal.

"Proportionate Share"
    Upon birth we're given
one mouth and two ears,
a wise man's usage
is a proportionate share.

Summer of '88

With a steadying hand I managed to walk.
With encouraging words you helped me to talk.
Each new day was a brand new slate.
I think it was the summer of '88.

Using the bathroom was a major event.
People watched over me wherever I went.
My food was scattered whenever I ate.
I think it was the summer of '88.

I'd suddenly chuckle and not know why.
For no special reason I'd break down and cry.
Surrounded by family monitoring my fate.
I think it was the summer of '88.

You'd think I was a toddler by the way that I act.
I can't remember names, or simple little facts.
The Golden Years of life were supposed to be great?
But not since the summer I turned 88.

Haiku
When the years behind
surpass the years remaining,
wisdom finds refuge.

"Daily Good"
Find a daily good and
you'll find daily happiness.

Perfect Dawn

The perfect dawn transpired from dusk
Feathered in laughter, candor and musk

A nervous encounter that quickly transformed
From trembling hands to a passionate storm

Our eyes couldn't hide what our hearts would see
As a spiritual gathering of 'meant to be's'

An absolute blend of woman and man
Seemingly drawn as destiny's plan

Yet still there's the question of 'Is it for real?'
For never before have we felt what we feel

We can only trust where our hearts might lead
Praying our emotions may forever be freed

Enormous obstacles together we'll shun
As our two kindred spirits mesh into one

For our hearts are aligned
amid a comforting calm
A perfect love
is at its perfect dawn.

Haiku
   Freedom of choice is either a privilege, or burden: it's your choice.

"Destiny"
   What some might see as "shouldn't be's", to others might be destiny.

Remember

Remember
love it might be fleeting,
but your heart will never lie.
If trust and respect are pillars,
then true love never dies.

Remember
those who throw daggers
at another man's pride,
Are often themselves aching
from daggers deep inside.

Remember
when parting with money,
help those who can't help themselves,
But for the lazy who choose regression,
keep your tithes unto yourself.

Remember
to follow a mentor
when following your own true heart,
And when it's your turn to mentor,
be sure to duly impart.

Remember
to respect the aged,
whether their minds are sound or not,
For when your years are fading,
you'll want the turn-a-bout.

Remember
to be a guiding light
to every youth you see,
And forgive their indiscretions,
Less you forget who you used to be.

Remember
to keep your riches
behind a pauper's shield,
And save them for the days
when the harvests refuse to yield.

Take pride in the daily expenses
when maintaining your humble abode,
For ignoring the tiny parcels,
might soon be a pachyderm's load.

May the friends
you keep be true ones,
and not selfishly their own,
And the love you show yourself,
to others may it also be shown.

If the path you think you're taking
is as wrong as you duly fear,
Just trust your inner compass,
for a new path starts right here.

Remember these things together,
in everything you do,
For when the good Lord comes calling
the world will remember you.

Haiku
*   I keep my friends close,*
but my enemies closer,
for they are within.

"Impasse"
*   Life's impasses can lead to your*
greatest rewards, or most painful regrets.
Wisdom is knowing whether to turn back,
or forge onward.

White Ceiling

I lay and I gaze
at a ceiling of white

Never changing in color
but I stare like it might

As if an answer
will magically appear

Solving my worries
and all of my fears

I know the answers
are not in the air

So with no alternatives
I'll just sit and stare

Haiku
   When dogs keep biting
a wise man realizes
stop petting the dogs.

"Rise Up"
   If I lose the fight
judge me not by the end,
for the real test
is if I rise up again.

Nonrefundable Gift

I received a gift that I couldn't return.
The more I used it the more I burned.

There are no directions on how it is used,
And most of the time the gift is abused.

At times it is wasted as I watch it just sit,
But it still grows in value the older I get.

When first I received it there seemed like a lot,
And the more I used it the wiser I got.

I can share it with others, or keep it all mine.
I wish I had more of this gift called...

"Time".

Haiku
*   I shall live my life*
like a great novel whose end
shall be penned by me.

"New Year's Magic"
*   The magic of New Years Day is*
how past failures transform into
new opportunities at a drop of a ball.

The Sentry

You guard a Coat of Arms
That bears our family name.
Carrying on traditions quietly without acclaim.

We rarely ever praised you for the goals that you had met,
For the challenges you've endured, for the examples you have set.

At times you seemed so distant, but now I understand
In fact you were only carrying the burdens of an honest man.

You delayed your personal dreams so we could pursue our own,
And challenged us as saplings. Your legacy as we've grown

Sometimes I think the mystery of the role that fathers play
Is veiled behind a shield to be revealed another day.

For not until I ventured into the world out on my own
Did I realize the "Sentry" in you was simply the love you've shown.

So how do I show my honor? Not in gold, nor in charms,
But in being just like you father,
And honoring our Coat of Arms.

Haiku
    Educated men
see the world with their own eyes
rather than other's.

        "Listen"
           Listen to what I'm saying,
        not to what you want to hear.

Our Song

In dreams as in life
In art as in song
There's a place in our hearts
Where loving souls belong

Like a Bedouin on a journey
An inner compass as his guide
We searched for something special
Inner voices we could not hide

They led us by the hand
To a place where love could start
By erasing painful memories
And opening loving hearts

Guiding us to a world
Where love was all along
Changing our skeptic spirits
Heightening our sense of song

So as we travel this journey
Crossing life's furrowed furlongs
Together we'll strike a chorus
As one we'll write "Our Song"

Haiku
    Some seek fortune, and
others seek fame, but most just
seek oblivion.

                      "Waves Goodbye"
                        Every time a child waves goodbye,
                        They fan their wings to help them fly.

Reversible Mirrors

My life's like a fun house
with reversible mirrors
Reflecting perfection
while hiding the errors

Of a life off track
like a derailed train
Projecting a smile
while hiding all the pain

And when you look inside
You will probably see
A reflection of you
and not really me

For reversible mirrors
protect what's inside
So you keep looking
and I'll continue to hide

Haiku
    Building yourself up
by burning others down leaves
you reeking of soot.

                              "Superior"
                If you think you're inferior then all will agree
                And no one can defend you if that's what you see
                Convince your mind to change your view
                And the superior person will be found in you

"Orangutan" - 15 x 20 watercolor painting. One of my favorite whimsical paintings. I wanted my toddler kids to participate on this painting, and you can see their hand prints as the red reeds in the grass. (2000)

Improbable Grace

Restoring my faith
seems an improbable task.
Disguising my sorrow
behind a jovial mask

Scarred from betrayal
and ultimate deceit
Gut wrenching turmoil
is my only receipt

As the internal decay
rips me apart
I no longer recognize
myself or my heart

My gift to me
so I might live:

"Forgive"

Haiku
   When you paint yourself pious, your canvas will soon be hypocrisy.

"Deceit"
   Friends retreat once you practice deceit.

Damned

Odin, dear Odin,
my loyal Grim Reaper.
Welcome our guests to their eternal keeper.

Valkyries to arms, and draw your white horses.
Hasten to silence these protagonist voices.

Take thy scythe and harvest their souls.
Listen through deaf ears their reasoning roles.
Capture their pleas in thy porous fists,
If only to dissipate through loosening grips.

Their prayers for mercy, are we expected to hear?
For only now have they bothered to share.
If not for the slamming of these cold metal doors,
They'd still be silent, but silent no more.

So Valkyries, dear Valkyries,
to arms for your Reaper.

Welcome our guests
to their eternal keeper.

Haiku
    The mute says nothing
when logic and reason fall
upon deaf men's ears.

"Inner Walls"
You can climb tall mountains,
and risk great falls,
But the greatest of climbs,
is your own inner walls.

Hold On

When the days are long
and you've reached your end
And you're searching your valley for strength again
When the hole you've dug has unscalable walls
And it's the last place on earth you wanted to fall
Hold On

When the cards you've been dealt can never be played
And your stoic appearance is just a charade
When faith has journeyed far from your soul
And you have yet to discover your meaningful role
Hold On

When your biggest regret is the life that you've made
And silence is the response to devotions you've prayed
Where fairness it seems is forever concealed
Have faith that an answer will soon be revealed, and
Hold On

When it comes to the pain you think you're alone
But the chasm you're crossing others have roamed
Find faith in the recess of your weary soul
Take comfort in knowing that God will console
And Hold On

Simply Hold On

Haiku
   *Shoulders carry weight
that pales in comparison
to a heavy heart.*

*"Happiness Way"
True happiness is not some
stop along the way;
it is the way.*

One Time

One drop
can start a river
One pebble
can start a landslide
One coin
can launch a fortune
One voice
can lead a nation
One act
can start a movement
One word
can heal a heart
One prayer
can restore a faith
One smile
can build a friendship
One friend
can change a life
One promise
can build a trust

One mistake can ruin it all

Haiku
    Would there not be a
mountain top if it weren't for
the valleys and plains?

"Charity"
    A charitable life worth begetting
Is receiving without forgetting,
And giving without expecting,
As if God you are reflecting.

"Wall Street" - 18 x 22 watercolor painting. Painted shortly after the stock market crash of 2008, it represents the strength of the "Bulls" as the "Bears" rear their ugly heads on occasion. My family's and pet's initials are captured as the background ticker symbols on the painting. (2008)

Definitions Change

My world envisioned
is now disarranged

And life's definitions
have certainly changed

So before you judge me
based on your views

Judge me not
less you've walked in my shoes

For life is not
as I planned it to be

And I'm not the person
I once knew as me

Haiku
*Sometimes a blind man
sees more clearly than a man
with perfect vision.*

*"Atheist"
I'd rather be perceived ignorant
by mortal atheists,
than confirmed ignorant
by an immortal God.*

"Victorian Peaks" - 15 x 18 watercolor painting. This painting captures a unique view of the Victorian Gazebo, and historic Courthouse on the Uptown Square of Medina, Ohio. (1999)

Butterflies on the Wind

From a sheltered cocoon
We long for the day
When our independence
Wisps us away
To face the challenges
Of an uncertain world
Anxious and fragile
With new wings unfurled

We climb upon winds
Knowing not where they lead
As they dictate a path
We're hastened to heed
Pirouetting atop
Of their powerful crests
Dancing on air
with a butterfly's zest

We often seek refuge
Among flowers or trees
Longing for shelter
In search of true peace
For sometimes the wind
Has a mind of it's own
And as dust clouds settle
We see we have grown

For the path we've "chosen"
Is really God's breeze
A struggling flight
Until we concede
That our destiny in life
Is really through Him
For until we do that
We're just

"Butterflies on the Wind"

Haiku
  Delicate, fragile,
beautiful; my heart is like
  a butterfly's wing.

"Time and Laughter"
  Time and laughter corrode
  the acerbic blade of deceit.

"Hidden Butterfly" - 24 x 30 acrylic painting. The painting is actually a mosaic of 80 smaller square paintings, of which 23 are hidden pictures; Killer Whale, Footprints, Presents, Newspapers, Birds Flying, Corn, Hummingbird Head, Baseball, Bikini Top, Tombstones, Highway, Frog Face, Glasses, Pac Man, Sunglasses and Face, Horse, Old Man Smoking, Batman Mask, Hop Scotch, Four Aces, Tear drops, Golf Ball, Smiley Face, and Kite. (2011)

Remember When

Remember when the darkness didn't have a light?
Remember when the blades of others actually cut?

Remember when your shouts were never heard?
Remember when you felt alone in a crowded room?

Remember when conversations never reached your ear?
Remember when your laugh was just a mask?

Remember when truths were just lies?
Remember when blankets were your only shields?

Remember when the tiniest victories made you cry?
Remember when the world could go to hell?

Remember when good news shielded bad?
Remember when the final blow wasn't the final?

Remember that friend who was there for you?
Remember?

Haiku

   *I found true freedom
when I became my own judge
rather than others'.*

"Children's Mirror"

   *When a child makes mistakes
we question their errors.
Could it be they don't listen,
or is it us that they mirror?*

"Jett & Gemini" - 11 x 14 watercolor painting. Rendition of the artist's horses drawn by the artist's 15 year old daughter. The artist had her paint most of it until the final touches. It was a procrastinated gift for the mom and wife that was started and completed on Christmas Eve. (2010)

Poppycock

Too much work
and not enough fun
They say that youth
is wasted on the young
"Poppycock" I say
for the time is here
to begin living life
as if you've no cares

I bequeath to the world
my worries and stress
deadlines, agendas,
and ultimate tests
Replace all of these
with frolic and fun
On my final marquee
put "Ornery One"

Before it all ends
discover what matters
Turn off the news
and political chatter
Think like a child
my daughters and sons
Life is too short
to not have fun

Haiku
　*It's tough hanging at
the equator, when others
bounce between their poles.*

"Clock"
　*A loss is not eminent,
nor victory a lock,
as long as you know
there is time on the clock.*

"Terminal Tower" - 20 x 30 watercolor painting. The Terminal Tower and Soldiers' and Sailors' Monument on the Cleveland Public Square. (2000)

Christmas Bells

Behold, a virgin with child, shall bring forth a Son.
They'll call his name Emmanuel, God with us" now as one.

The star had led the shepherds to the place where Jesus lay.
A savior born in Bethlehem, upon a Christmas Day
The wise men that had followed to witness this holy place.
Knelt before the true king, humbled in his grace.

(Refrain) Ring the bells ye faithful, ring both far and near.
Ring the bells ye faithful, ring for all to hear.
The babe He is our shepherd, and our one true king
So ring the bells ye faithful, let the bells all ring.

The choirs of angels trumpet, proclaiming to the world
Born this day's a savior, a gift of grace unfurled
Fall to your knees in glory, for all to humbly pray.
For blessed are the faithful, upon this Christmas Day.
(Refrain)

The Virgin Mother Mary, and Joseph the family sire
Endured the scorn of others, for belief in something higher
Their Child, He changed the world, upon his humble birth.
Revealing a path to heaven, and peace to all on earth.
(Refrain)

As man would soon discover, the errors of his ways
And find a place of solace, in His Christmas grace
For God so loved his people, hearing their pleading calls
He brought his Son before us, the greatest gift of all.
(Refrain)

Haiku
    Opinions often
are mass produced with little
quality control.

"*Shhhhh*"
    Peace can be heard
only through silence.

"Duomo, Florence, Italy" - 12 x 18 watercolor painting. A Christmas gift for my daughter on her return from a life-changing college study abroad trip to Florence, Italy. (2016)

Kiss on the Cheek

Each night we'd whisper as I tucked you in.
A laugh, a giggle, a poke on the chin,
A toss of the covers as we played hide-n-seek,
A final "goodnight" with a kiss on the cheek.

Under the silence of twilight I'd always return,
For a prayer of my own and the lessons I've learned.
Not for great victories or fortunes of kings,
But for God to bless you with the simplest of things.

Like the peace of knowing your purpose on Earth.
That you'd always marvel at the miracle of birth.
To cherish your family as God's loving gift,
And give unto Him your burdens to lift.

To pause and remember to take it all in.
To wipe away tears with the kindness of friends.
And cherish the music of each child's laugh,
While finding forgiveness for pains of the past.

For soon the sun sets and the light starts to fade,
And you long for more of the life that you've made.
To pause and turn for that one final peek.
A loving "goodnight" and a kiss on the cheek.

Haiku
My life's therapist
is music, it's medicine
great lyrics and dance.

"Dive In"
You can't swim with the sharks
while floating on an ark

"Toledo, Spain" - 12 x 18 watercolor painting. A Christmas gift for my son on his return from a life-changing college study abroad trip to Toledo, Spain. (2016) The poem "Kiss on the Cheek" was written for a friend facing her own twilight in life who wanted to pass on her life's lessons to her kids, who are now raising their own families.

Country Air

A passing smile in a high school hall
A few more times and soon I'd fall
I found my dream while still so young
There was no doubt she was the one
And friends would ask how could it be
That I knew she was the one for me

She won me over with her heather blues
Her smile reminds me of a sunset hue
Her heart's as soft as her Aspen hair
She's my breath, my country air

In later years my script in life
Turned a chapter when she became my wife
Two souls as one we both would be
A life together just her and me
As her veil was lifted on our wedding day
Turning to me her dad would say

She won me over with her heather blues
Her smile reminds me of a sunset hue
Her heart's as soft as her Aspen hair
She's my breath, my country air
(continued)

As the seasons passed our lives we'd share
With a blue eyed daughter with golden hair
A deeper love; an answered prayer
We needed her as we needed the air
There'll come a day she'll walk the aisle
And I'll say to the groom with a tear and a smile

She won me over with her heather blues
Her smile reminds me of a sunset hue
Her heart's as soft as her Aspen hair
She's my breath, my country air

<u>"Little Lady"</u> - 14 x 22 watercolor painting. The painting is a portrait of the artist's eight-month old daughter on a family picnic, while thinking she was "all that" in her designer hat. It is a hat that will always remain a remembrance of simpler times. (1998). "Country Air" was a song I wrote for my daughter when she asked me to write one for her.

About the Author

Richard Doyle is a byproduct of his Midwestern upbringing. Born in Cleveland Heights, Ohio, in 1964, he was the third youngest of nine kids in a typical Irish Catholic home. He would later move with his family at the age of four to the quintessential "hometown" of Medina, Ohio. From there he'd stay until leaving for college, and eventually settling down to raise his own family just down the road in Wadsworth, Ohio, with his wife and two kids.

As an active youth he was focused more on sports than on art. As a senior, he was a three sport athlete, but somehow managed to find time to participate in the "Arts" as an actor in his high school play "The Matchmaker", and as a Russian dancer in the musical "Fiddler on the Roof". He never took an art class in high school.

Richard graduated with a degree in Business Administration - Finance from The Ohio State University, which was not an easy road for him. His father passed away shortly after he graduated from high school. He worked his way through college in what ended up being one of his most difficult challenges, but also his most rewarding. Having been the first of his siblings to graduate from college, he would later go on to establish a successful financial services firm where he remains today.

An accomplished speaker, Richard enjoys speaking in front of groups of all sizes in both public and private settings. He enjoys sharing his life experiences with audiences of all ages.

Richard prides himself on the diversity of his work; not only with his visual arts, but also his literary works. You never know where his next project will lead him. His works of art are on display in prominent locations throughout the region. He looks at his works as a legacy that generations can enjoy for years to come.

Unique Legacies

1. "Medina County Lifestyle Magazine" article March 2017 2. "Because they Came" cover art 2011
3. Sisters of Notre Dame 2014 Calendar 4. Medina Sun Times article 5. Ohio National Guard care package card for Afghanistan 2008 6. Medina High School Special Needs joint project with Medina Bee Statues for Keller Williams 7. Medina City Council retirement gifts 8. Medina High School special needs class project "Combined Talents Lincoln Mosaic" 9. Sacred Heart of Jesus Elementary School mural with the kids participation.

Signature Historic Collage Series

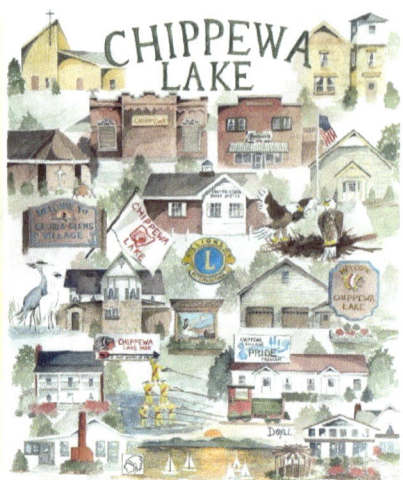

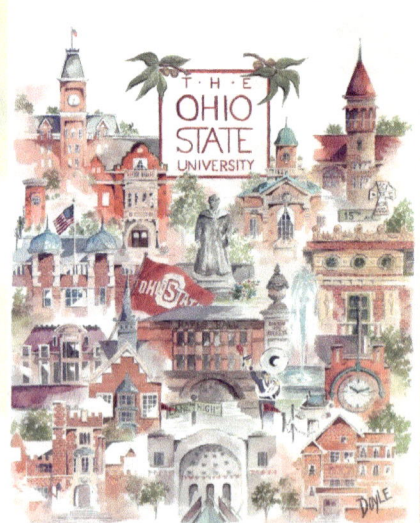

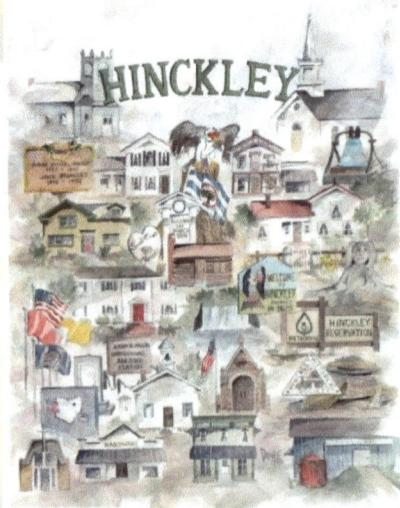

Original Painting Locations

"Ohio University Collage"	Schoonover Bldg, Scripps College, Ohio University, Athens, Ohio
"Ohio State Collage"	Alumni Office, The Ohio State University, Columbus, Ohio
"Grandville Ohio Collage"	Grandville Inn, Grandville, Ohio
"Hinckley Ohio Collage"	Hinckley Township Hall, Hinckley, Ohio
"Valley City Ohio Collage"	Rail Road Depot Museum, Valley City, Ohio
"Wadsworth Ohio Collage"	Wadsworth City Hall and Municipal Building, Wadsworth, Ohio
"Medina Collage"	Medina City Hall, Medina, Ohio
"Chatham Bicentennial"	Chatham Historical Town Hall, Chatham, Ohio
"Westfield Bank"	Westfield Bank Home Office, Westfield Center, Ohio
"Medina Townships"	Medina Probate Court House Office, Medina, Ohio
"Medina Justice"	Judge Kevin Dunn Chambers, Medina Court House, Medina, Ohio
"Sharon Center Collage"	St. Paul Lutheran Church, Sharon Center, Ohio
"Cleveland Clinic"	Cleveland Clinic Regional V.P. Office (Location unknown) Ohio
"Medina Hospital"	Cleveland Clinic Medina Hospital CEO Office, Medina, Ohio
"North Ridgeville Collage"	North Ridgeville Chamber of Commerce (private collector) Ohio
"Little Whiz"	Little Whiz Fire Museum, Medina, Ohio
"Alber Farm Collage"	Darren and Holly Alber Personal Collection, Las Vegas, Nevada
"Sisters of Notre Dame"	Sisters of Notre Dame Home Office, Chardon, Ohio
"Castle Ansell"	Sisters of Notre Dame Home Office, Chardon, Ohio
"Brunswick Collage"	Heritage Farm Museum, Brunswick Historical Society Ohio
"Western Reserve Bank"	Western Reserve Bank CEO Private Collection, Medina, Ohio
"Forest City Technologies"	John Cloud, Owner Forest City Technologies, Wellington, Ohio
"Chippewa Lake Collage"	Chippewa Lake Town Hall, Chippewa Lake, Ohio
"Victorian Peaks"	Morse Family Private Collection, Medina, Ohio
"Gazebo Flowers"	Morse Family Private Collection, Lauderdale by the Sea, Florida
"Orangutan"	Hyest Family Private Collection, Powell, Ohio
"Duomo, Florence Italy"	Kathryn Doyle Private Collection, Wadsworth, Ohio
"Toledo, Spain"	Matthew Doyle Private Collection, Wadsworth, Ohio
"Giraffe"	Private Collection, Medina, Ohio (location unknown)
"Sacred Heart Church"	Winkler Family Private Collection, Wadsworth, Ohio
"Lincoln Mosaic"	Medina High School Special Needs Class Hallway, Medina, Ohio
"Jesus Wept"	Jane Twohey Private Collection, Port Perry, Ontario, Canada
"Medina County Bicentennial"	County Administration Building, Medina, Ohio
"Gators National Guard"	Ohio National Guard Armory, Medina, Ohio
"Taj Mahal"	Chinmaya Vijaya Orphanage, Vijayawada, India
"Jesus With Children"	Mural in Sacred Heart School, Wadsworth, Ohio
"Medina Gazebo"	Lucy Sondles, Leadership Medina County Office, Medina, Ohio
"Hooligan's Irish Pub"	Hooligan's Irish Pub, Put-In-Bay, Ohio

www.ingramcontent.com/pod-product-compliance
Lightning Source LLC
Chambersburg PA
CBHW042008150426
43195CB00002B/53